The Rainbow Series of
To Touch The Heart

For Elsie,
With love,
Chrissy Greenslade

RAINBOW OF THE HEART

Rainbow of The Heart   *Book Two*

Poetry by Chrissy Greenslade.
Illustrations by Josephine Winzar.

PETRA PUBLISHING

RAINBOW OF THE HEART

ISBN: 0-9534319-1-6

First Edition published Spring 2000 by
PETRA PUBLISHING
4, Leven Close
Bournemouth
BH4 9LP

> " *I dedicate this book to Cliff,*
> *For love and encouragement in this world,*
> *And to Dendy for love and encouragement from the next.*
> *Also to all those who need love and encouragement.* "

Also by Chrissy Greenslade:
Rainbow of Life

British Library Cataloguing in Publication Data:
A catalogue record for this book is available from the British Library

Printed in China through World Print Ltd.

Layout & Design Mark A Fudge

CONTENTS

ACKNOWLEDGEMENTS

The following poems of mine have previously been published in the following magazines and annuals.

The People's Friend

Maxie
Travelling Light
Squoosh
April

The Science of Thought Review

Achievement
Reach out for the light

The Fireside Book

Breakfast in Bed
Serenade to Squirrels
Spring Cleaning

The Daily Echo

Never too Late

The Lady

River Meadows

Secrets

True or False

The People's Friend Annual

Leisure

The Journal (DHWSHA)

Cindy

Inspire

You don't have to be perfect to be good

New Vision

Hold On
My Beatitudes

INTRODUCTION

Over the past year, I have received tremendous happiness, by the reactions, letters and comments, from the readers of my first book, 'Rainbow of Life.' So it is with the greatest pleasure, that I bring you the second book of the Rainbow Series, 'Rainbow of the Heart.'

A favourite comment made to me by a lady, who had been given the book by her husband was, "I don't particularly like poetry and I would never have bought a poetry book myself but I really loved your book. I sat at breakfast reading out some of your poems. We had a real laugh at the funny ones, and the others were so true to life."

Many people were moved by the spiritual poems, which had a special meaning for them. I'm so happy that poems from my book have been read at concerts, talks, churches and even at a wedding! Also six of the poems from my first book have been translated into Albanian and included in a collection of poems.

My poetry is based on my life or experiences I have known. I am sure, as in the first book, you will identify with many of my poems. God continues to work with my gift of poetry, as He does with Josephine and her beautiful, inspired illustrations. This book could not have been produced without Mark, the other part of our wonderful team. It is a book created in harmony and we hope that it will bring something special into your lives.

As I've said previously, I make no profit but want only to share my gift of writing and especially the love and comfort my book contains. As I said in 'Rainbow of Life,' if only one poem touches you or gives your life new meaning, then in this book I will have succeeded.

In this series of books. I share with you the feelings in my heart, which make up the rainbow of my life. Once again, hand in hand, cross over the rainbow with me.

Love and Light, Chrissy.

For further information, book requirements, poetry readings and talks please contact
Chrissy Greenslade, Petra Publishing, 4 Leven Close, Bournemouth BH4 9LP
Tel: 01202 762730   E-mail address: cgreenslade@petrarainbow.freeserve.co.uk
Internet website address: http://www.petrarainbow.freeserve.co.uk

MAXIE

Brown are the eyes
Of my dearest companion,
Winning his ways
And the wag of his tail,
Trusting his eyes,
Filled with love and devotion,
Offered paw, licks,
Melt my heart, cannot fail.

Thump on the bed,
Here's my morning alarm clock,
Anxiously waits
For his breakfast to start,
Newspaper, slippers,
Triumphant he carries,
Welcomes me home,
With a warm, joyful heart.

Loud is the bark
As my protector warns me,
Joyful his 'Woof'
As he asks for his lead.
Swift are the feet
Of my hunter and athlete,
Energy fired,
Now that he has been freed.

Lying his head
On my feet he's contented,
Opening one eye,
When pretending to sleep,
I am so glad
That one day I decided,
This was the dog,
-No one wanted - I'd keep.

TRAVELLING LIGHT

It only was for five days,
The packing took me two,
There seemed so much to think about,
So many things to do.

Thin clothes in case it's warmer,
Warm clothes I took galore,
I struggled to zip up the case,
Guilt feelings to the fore.

"You won't need many changes,
It's not for very long",
But pushing in a party dress,
I hope to prove him wrong.

I have such good intentions,
To be spartan and good,
But slipping in my dancing shoes,
I took more than I should.

It could be cold in Autumn,
Bed jacket for the night,
Of course it was extremely warm,
Why can't I get things right?

I put my dressy jacket,
To brighten up my trews,
Some blouses and two cardigans,
Such problems which I'd use.

My hubby is so easy,
Trousers and shirts and ties,
It isn't what he takes with him,
Which causes all my sighs.

When finally I unpacked,
Inside the hotel room,
I gave a cry of horror for
I could see problems loom.

He hasn't packed his razor,
I've put in his wrong shoes,
I think I'll make some tea before
I tell him the bad news!

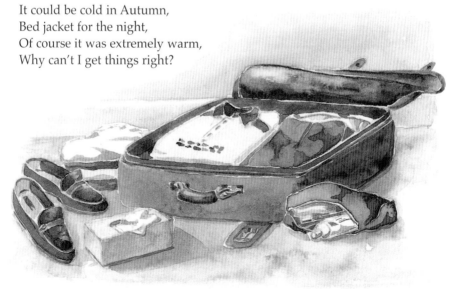

ACHIEVEMENT

It's the effort that's made that's important,
Not succeeding the very first time,
It's the fact that you're trying to get there,
And the height of the mountain you climb.

It's your positive thoughts that accomplish,
And the hope in your heart kept alight,
It's the motive, the purpose, the progress,
Which persuades you, 'Don't give up the fight.'

For the toddler his joy is the first step,
For a youth it is passing his test,
For a man when he gets his first pay rise,
For a bride when she's feathered her nest.

For a drug addict and alcoholic,
It is learning to give up what's bad,
For a stroke victim it is recovering
Power of speech and the movement they had.

But a smile too can be an achievement,
When a loss is destroying your soul,
And a will to live on, if disabled,
When the people around you are whole.

To be able to dress, learn to do things,
Which you couldn't have achieved before,
To read braille and to master sign language,
Or to simply get up from the floor.

To achieve there must always be helpers,
A good teacher, a doctor, a friend,
So be positive for God is helping,
And you'll find you will cope in the end.

BREAKFAST IN BED

Breakfast in bed on a dull Sunday morning,
Brown toast and white toast, a sweet cup of tea,
Smiling I survey the male decoration,
That's brought with such love
From my darling for me.

Tall flask and small flask and uncovered teapot,
Traycloth is missing, no milk jug in sight,
Crumpled the napkin, delicious the moment,
The toast is still hot
As I now take a bite.

Sated I survey my now empty lunch plate,
On which my scraped toast was thoughtfully laid,
Secretly smiling, I thank him, won't tell him,
That I wrote an ode
On how it was displayed!

SERENADE TO SQUIRRELS

Squirrels in the tree tops,
Flying through the air,
Squirrels in the garden,
Squirrels everywhere.

They scamper through the woodland,
And creep along the fence,
Climb swiftly up high tree trunks,
Food hunting, so intense.

Frustrated over bird food,
Caged neatly out of reach,
For nuts they strive and struggle,
And hang on like a leech.

Then in traditional poses,
They nibble seeds and such,
And look so sweet and pretty,
I love them very much.

Although they eat the blossoms,
And nip camellia heads,
In spite of vicious history
Of killing all the reds;

I love their frisky manner,
Their tails flashed through with white,
Their playful, cute behaviour,
As they race out of sight.

Some call them pests, a nuisance,
As they live wild and free,
But oh, how much I'd miss them,
If they didn't live with me.

NOT SUCH A NITWIT

My friend had such a problem
Since her husband had retired,
He couldn't settle, moped about,
Felt dull and uninspired.

In summer it was easy
With the garden chores outside,
But once the cold, dark days arrived,
This pleasure was denied.

He tried his model-making
As he'd done when in his youth,
But fingers weren't so nimble if
He'd only tell the truth.

T.V. writing, and puzzles,
Every kind of game he tried,
But giving up, quite miserable,
He drooped around and sighed.

His wife frustrated watched him,
So dejected, grumpy, sitting,
"Instead of doing nothing Dear,
Do help me with my knitting?"

Wool, knitting pins and patterns,
Now all clutter up the place,
But pleasure and contentment lie
Upon his beaming face.

His skill is quite amazing,
Knitted clothes they have galore,
His wife is so delighted for
He's busy and what's more -

Her knitting isn't needed,
In her eye there is a gleam,
Those fascinating night-classes
No longer are a dream.

She longs to wield a spanner
As she hasn't clothes to knit,
Time now to learn a language for
She's often fancied it.

A score of Courses beckon,
So she says as she is looking,
"If I learn car mechanics Dear,
Would you like to do some cooking?

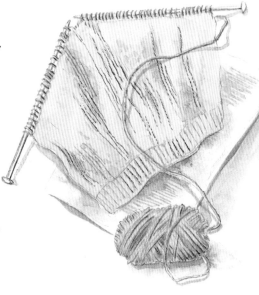

DON'T RESIST

Accept the things that come your way,
Don't fight them or you'll find,
That they'll get worse and out of hand,
As tension fills your mind.

Accept but first seek God's advice,
Ask Him to share your task,
You'll find support, right answers, strength,
The moment that you ask.

Accept, don't ask "Why should this be?"
Each happening is a test,
For life on earth's a place to learn
The way to live the best.

Accept the sorrows and the pain,
For through them we progress,
They'll lead to patience, courage, trust,
And inner happiness.

Accept that God is by your side,
That if your thoughts are good,
You'll help yourself and lead your life,
Exactly as you should.

NEVER TOO LATE.

As I flicked through 'The Echo,'
Cast here and there a glance,
Three words caught my attention,
'Adults' and then 'Tap Dance.'

My heart it gave a quiver,
Westbourne was its venue,
How close it was, how handy,
My dream it might come true.

I rushed rang 'Happy Tapping,'
And quickly made a date,
To trip the light fantastic,
Before it was too late.

So keen I arrived early,
Joined other ladies there,
Hoping I'd not look stupid,
Cause anyone to stare.

But how I envied others,
Who wore tap dancing shoes,
That silver sound of magic,
But black! Not what I'd choose.

We shuffled, hopped and side-stepped,
As childhood dreams came true,
My right foot - great! My left foot?
Didn't do as it should do.

Sometimes my concentration
Completely slipped away,
But for this 'Shirley Temple,'
This hour had made her day.

I tap-danced in the car-park ,
And tap-danced to the door,
I tap-danced in the hallway,
And on the bathroom floor.

It's given me such pleasure,
And laughs too I must mention,
How good to feel like 'Ginger,'
When I go to fetch my pension!

RIVER MEADOWS

The swifts and martins darted,
Sleek-winged above my head,
A starling baby pestered,
Beak gaping to be fed.

A swan on mighty nest-throne,
Arranged her downy wings,
A humpy bridge, cow-parsleyed,
A thousand living things.

A path bewitched by beeches,
With gnarled and knotted arms,
Where robin-hood and burdock,
And birds-eye flaunt their charms.

As water's sleeping movements,
Sway weeds and cress and flowers,
Bright insects fish and moorhen,
Spend happy sun-splashed hours.

A meadow massed with buttercups,
A heron's swift descent,
These gave to me, this day in May,
The happiest hours I've spent.

SQUOOSH

I love to eat an orange,
But I get it on my face,
Right up my nose and on my clothes,
It shoots 'way into space.

The drips they stain my trousers,
But it's such a lovely smell,
It's nice and sweet and good to eat,
But makes my daddy yell.

"Be careful how you eat it,
Now it's shot right in my eye."
I suck and suck but with my luck,
The juice goes flying by.

And when with juicy fingers,
I take hold of Mummy's hand,
She pulls a face, what a disgrace,
I cannot understand.

I only ate an orange,
But this no-one can abide,
For I confess I make a mess,
Next time I'll go outside!

YOU DON'T HAVE TO BE PERFECT TO BE GOOD

I'm singing and happy this morning,
I feel so much peace in my heart,
With joy brimming over I chuckle,
I can't wait for this new day to start.

I suddenly know I've succeeded,
My longing for peace has returned,
And now my emotions are steady,
I have found the contentment I yearned.

I know that each day holds a challenge,
A lesson to learn for my gain,
But now I can calmly approach it,
For my role in this life is quite plain.

I really don't have to be perfect,
The way that I am God loves me,
So now I can stop feeling guilty,
And must love the real me and be free.

Then when I slip up, and feel sorry,
Retorts from my quick tongue have tripped,
I know that for sure I'm forgiven,
Though my 'halo' as usual has slipped.

For because I am trying to be good,
I feel so much love all around,
And now I accept that this 'angel',
Will quite often fall flat on the ground.

I sing as I smile in the bath tub,
Let happy thoughts push out the sad,
Today I'm so glad I'm an 'angel,'
When I fail next I'll not feel so bad!

THE EYE OF THE BEHOLDER

I wonder if Eve was made perfect,
Or was she unusual at all,
Because all we females are different,
Some skinny, some plump and some tall?

The fair sex have never accepted,
Their differences make them unique,
For long necks, plump bodies, thin models,
Great artists deliberately seek.

If tiny we hanker for tallness,
If bonny we wish we were thin,
We never are really contented,
With the size or the shapes we are in.

If hair is short, blonde, very curly,
How nice if it's long, dark and straight,
We change both its style and the colour,
Resisting both time and our fate.

Remember again our great artists,
Who chose a particular kind,
And called them goddesses and beauties
Ideas of perfection in mind.

Be grateful just smile and be thankful.
Good features you know you possess,
Make light of so-called imperfections,
Just forget them and find happiness.

LEISURE

I thought today would be the best,
A free day full of joy and rest,
I put my hands behind my head,
Enjoying Sunday's lie in bed.

Perhaps I'd walk down to the sea,
Sit in the garden with my tea,
A picnic or a gentle hike,
A lazy ride upon the bike?

Which one to choose? I must decide,
I throw the curtains open wide,
I see the rain upon the pane,
And jump back into bed again.

THOUGHTS ON A MOTHER

Mothers are so commonplace,
Too numerous to name,
They're there because of you and me,
And claim no right to fame.
They vary in their sizes,
In the happiness they give,
They affect every part of us,
Also the way we live.

They give us our first breath of life,
The first warmth that we feel,
The arms and love surrounding us,
Are tender, strong and real;
They are our comforters, our food,
Our darkness and our light,
They are the breasts we snuggle on,
The face that we first sight.

Throughout the years their hand is there,
To lift us when we fall,
They are the ones who come to us,
When in the dark we call.
They take away our doubts and fears,
And make us feel so brave,
They show us how to play and learn,
And how we should behave.

As we grow big and problems start,
We find we're lost and weak,
They then provide the good advice,
The loving that we seek.
They are the ones we hurt the most,
Because we're immature,
But it's our mother who forgives,
Whose love for us is sure.

When we rebel at sound advice,
Because of youth and greed,
We cause much sadness, pain and tears,
Which mothers do not need,
But once we've grappled with our youth,
And grown in heart and mind,
We understand the mother who
Is loving, sweet and kind.

We know when times were needed
When she had to shout or scold,
We see with sudden shock and fear,
That soon she will be old.
This dear, sweet mother who has been,
The world to you and me,
Her thoughtful ways, her love and care,
She's given readily.

She's worked and prayed and worried,
And looked after us each day,
And now it's time that in our life,
Some love we can repay.
We'll give to her a helping hand,
A kind word and a smile,
Know when she's tired or feeling ill,
And comfort her a while.

Now is the time she needs to feel,
Relaxed and loved and free,
Because she has someone who cares,
Someone like you and me!
And when it is her time to leave
This earth, for her new start,
We'll always be together for
We'll hold her in our heart.

ABSOLUTION

If we link with God and sit and pray,
If we are sincere in things we say,
If we want to keep bad thoughts at bay,
Turn to God.

When we're full of guilt for things we've done,
When the clouds of doubt cover the sun,
When we feel we can't face anyone,
Turn to God.

If we've failed but know we've tried our best,
If our patience doesn't pass the test,
If our good intentions have gone west,
Turn to God.

When bad tempers flare and get the better,
When we've failed to phone or write a letter,
When possessions tend to bind and fetter,
Turn to God.

If we turn to God and ask the way,
If we've had a difficult, tiring day,
If it's "Sorry" that we're trying to say,
We're forgiven.

When we try next time to curb our tongue,
Tolerance now shown with old and young,
When instead of grumbling, praise is sung,
We're forgiven.

If we keep a promise to a friend,
If we post that card we meant to send
If we really do what we intend,
We're forgiven.

When with God we start and end our day,
Using His support to pave the way,
It is sheer relief that we can say,
We're forgiven.

BARGAIN BOOSTER

We can't resist a bargain,
A 'Buy one get one free,'
That's why we have six quiches,
Too many cakes for tea.

Why does this pie taste better,
It's flavour really nice?
Is it because this meat pie,
Was bought at half the price?

We sometimes get excited,
By quantity and size,
And stare at tempting bargains,
With disbelieving eyes,

For we have seen the package,
The box so big and wide,
But find the packet's double,
The quantities inside.

Sometimes goods are outdated,
Not aged but have expired,
The aerosol that seemed cheap,
Has scent no one desired.

Be choosy with your bargains,
Consider carefully,
Or you'll over-load your freezer,
With your 'Buy one get one free.'

APRIL

April is a white-massed hedge,
Snow-blossom of Blackthorn,
Increasing chorus of songbirds,
Excited by the dawn.

Returning martins swoop and rest,
Plump fruit buds grow and swell,
The Brimstone and the bumble-bee,
Alight where flowers dwell.

Fleet, aerobatic lapwings flirt
In bursts of springtime sun,
And noisy coots and moorhens chase
In courtship and in fun.

The sound of cuckoo's impudence,
Makes flowering cherries blush;
On hunting, twig-collecting trips,
Go robin, wren and thrush.

The scent of fresh, mown lawn-cuttings,
The promise of the Spring,
April for me has hope itself,
Contained in everything.

JUST 'WEIGHT.'

I've stood upon the weighing scales,
And seen to my dismay,
The kilos zooming far too high,
I'm more than I should weigh.

I resolve at that moment that
I'll take myself in hand,
And when I'm offered creamy cakes,
Make a determined stand.

My trousers do feel much too tight,
My tummy far too rounded,
How fast I put the inches on,
I really am astounded.

At breakfast I am smug for I've
Had cereal and fruit,
And walking past the biscuit tin,
I didn't give a hoot.

I felt so proud at two o'clock,
After my salad lunch,
I feel this time I can be strong,
When I've the urge to munch.

At five o'clock I'm feeling parched,
So make a cup of tea,
I take the fruit cake from the fridge,
Oh, how it's tempting me.

It's just a slip, but suppertime,
I need a little snack,
I make it carbohydrate free,
Pat myself on the back.

I'm alright till I watch T.V.
I must confess with sorrow,
I've eaten a whole chocolate bar,
I'll start again tomorrow!

IN TIME OF TROUBLE

It takes courage to really hand over,
And believe that another knows best,
It's not easy to let go of fear,
But it's God putting us to the test.

Now's the time to accept it's the right time,
To hand over yourself to the Lord,
For His love and His healing and power,
Is still there though it's often ignored.

So accept that His angels are with you,
That your guardians surround you with light,
That His care is the care of a father,
That it's His arms now holding you tight.

Then with faith, filled with hope and with comfort,
You will face all that's lying ahead,
With the knowledge and peace that He hears you,
All your thoughts and the prayers that are said.

So God bless you, and dear friend I'm sending
On swift wings, healing prayers in the light,
For I know they are heard, wrapped around you,
And that everything will be alright.

MYSTERY AT THE HAIRDRESSERS

I thought that I had seen the lot,
- I turned the switch to medium hot -
But when I looked and saw her there,
Embarrassed, twitching in her chair,
I laughed and laughed until I cried,
If I was her I would have died.
They'd put a helmet on her head,
Much worse than nets some wear
  in bed.

A rubber, fireman helmet hat,
With holes in it? Just fancy that!
Then through a hole they pulled a strand
Of hair. I was in wonderland.
I'd never seen a sight like this,
I didn't want a thing to miss.
Over her eyes the rubber flap,
Added more humour to the cap.

Then lots of tint which looked
  like paint,
Or custard cream - I thought I'd faint
If it was me in that dire state,
I'd not have survived such a fate.
I watched. A hood and towel
  were wrapped
Around her head, arabian capped,
Then peeping, pulling strands of hair,
Assistants huddled 'round her chair.

At first a spikey Boadicea,
Now arab, soon it would be clear
What the results of this would be,
With baited breath I longed to see.
Oh dear, my hair will soon be dry,
How quickly has the time gone by;
Will I find out? They've peeped again!
Will it a mystery remain?

But after seeing all that mess,
What could be possible I guess.
Is something special, daring, bright,
Oh I do hope that I am right.
Out of the cap she has been taken,
She's being washed. Am I mistaken?
I see no difference from before,
What were the spikes and cream
  pie for?

She's being dried then rollered up,
Now sipping from her coffee cup;
But as I'll miss the final show,
I must ask what I need to know.
"Oh, she has had her highlights done."
That's what it was! It's not much fun
For her, but really I must say,
It was the highlight of my day!

FRUITS OF WAR

He rocked in his chair as he thought of the war,
Of the suffering and pain he had seen,
Now he smiled at the comfort, his books and T.V.
At his life so secure and serene.

At sixteen he'd told them that he was of age,
Keenly proud to join up with the men,
In a few, cruel months as he saw his pals die,
What a boy, not a man he felt then.

Recalling the tiredness, rain-drenched, deep in mud,
Icy cold, such vile stench and the dread,
He remembered stark fear and his screams and the noise,
As they shot him and left him for dead.

The enemy found him - through youth he was saved,
So they nursed him and brought back his life,
And amongst all those nurses an angel stood there,
Then much later he made her his wife.

He smiled across now at her beautiful face,
Where the love in her eyes still shone bright;
But the irony was she'd have never been there,
If her kinsmen he'd not had to fight!

TRUE OR FALSE

He couldn't understand it for
They said it wasn't bad,
To master teeth that weren't his own,
He really would be glad.

But no-one had pre-warned him that
His tastebuds would be lost,
His mouth feel full of marbles for
A most outrageous cost.

I didn't try to force him as
His plate held only four,
But wearing them he was again,
The man that I adore.

He really didn't like them though
He tried them for a while,
For soon he took them out again,
And gave a tight-lipped smile.

So now I am resigned because
I want to see him happy,
I love him as he is right now,
Both comfortable and gappy.

And as I didn't know till now,
With them he couldn't whistle,
I'm glad to hear his favourite tune,
As I end my sad epistle.

REACH OUT FOR THE LIGHT

The light of God
Is like sun on your face,
It fills you with warmth,
And with loving and grace.
It mellows, relaxes
Your body and soul,
It's comforting, healing,
And makes you feel whole.

Surrender then,
Really reach for the centre,
You wait, for you know
Soon that God's light will enter.
Reach out now and grasp it,
And bathe in its source,
As questions are answered,
You'll take the right course.

If now and then,
You feel you've lost the way,
Just listen and hear
What your still voice will say.
Rejoice in the sunlight,
God's love, in the Spring,
For bathed in His light you
Can face anything.

SPOILT FOR CHOICE

I couldn't make my mind up,
For there was so much to see,
Fine plants all shapes and sizes,
Arrayed in front of me.

I halted at hydrangeas,
Then I sorted through the shrubs,
I looked at trees and pot plants,
At conifers in tubs.

The primulas were pretty,
I quite fancied one or two,
I saw a unique lily,
A lovely shade of blue.

I read heights of perennials,
Orientals I admired,
But couldn't make my mind up,
Which one I most desired.

Bewildered and exhausted,
Finally I chose some blooms,
Both colourful and cheerful,
They'd brighten up my rooms.

I clutched my gay, silk flowers,
Hoping folk would still be kind,
As they knew I'd wanted live ones,
But I'd made up my mind.

They wouldn't need attention,
Fertiliser, peat or lime,
I love my man-made flowers,
I'll choose real ones next time!

JANUARY WALK

Ice cold the day, frozen the hedge,
Leaves icing-sugar coated,
The fields are dressed in virgin best,
Where soft snow flakes have floated.

The ice-grey pools with cracking face,
Resist boot-laden footfalls,
Stark, umber trees, frost-laden breeze,
Red berries glow on stone walls.

Grey whisps of smoke amongst
  the trees,
To wintry skies ascending,
Rich russet larches, bearded arches,
Stream floods in meadows wending.

A squirrel hunts for hidden nuts,
A rook, sheen-coated searches
Furrows that steam, as sea gulls scream,
Whilst skimming fragile birches.

A winter's day, all warmed with sun,
Although our faces tingle,
A quickened pace, a freezing face,
Our breath and frost-air mingle.

We stamp our feet, remove our gloves,
And enter, hunger growing,
Such warmth and light, cosy delight,
The hearth coals still are glowing.

We shed our coats, make cups of tea,
Now apple logs smell spicy,
With outstretched toes, our
  warm blood flows,
To limbs no longer icy.

In fireside chair, with buttered toast,
Our cheeks now flushed and rosy,
We both agree wholeheartedly,
January can be cosy.

SPRING CLEANING

At last we've had a spring-clean,
The attic is now bare,
And all that's left are odds and ends,
Some cupboards and a chair.

We feel triumphant, happy,
That all our junk is moved,
A twenty-five year clear-out,
Was possible we've proved.

But now the shed is bulging,
Outside the house a mess,
The overcrowded garage is
A problem we confess.

Because it's to be sorted,
The place is like a tip,
We've postponed further moving,
Until we hire a skip.

It's not the actual clearing,
But what to throw away,
For things might come in handy so,
We'll leave them for today.

HOLD ON

When you struggle and fret,
And your mind's not at rest,
You are facing once more,
Yet another life's test.

When your peace is disturbed
By your thoughts which run riot,
Don't you find it so hard
To stay tranquil and quiet?

When your heart's seeking God,
But He's not to be found,
When it's hard to unite
With your friends all around;

When things just don't seem right,
You feel lost in your mind,
It is then in despair,
That God's strength you will find.

So relax and still seek,
Reaching out for the light,
For it's only a moment
That God's out of your sight.

Just hold on, persevere,
When you want to give in,
And then comfort you'll find,
As your peace will begin.

DORSET CREAM TEA

Wielding our walking sticks
One sunny Sunday,
To the tea garden
We joyfully went,
Licking our lips, now
Our taste buds excited,
A tasty cream tea was
A special event.

*Rounding the corner both
Laughing and hungry,
Blessed were our eyes
At the sight we could see,
Dripping with flowers,
Bright butterflies flitting,
With spotless lawn tables
Arranged for our tea.*

*Lashings of jam, rich with
Plump, scrumptious strawberries,
Cream thick and clotted,
Not puffed from a can,
Scones warm to handle,
As fresh as your mum made,
That's what I shared with
My own darling man.*

Some folks ate crumpets,
Just oozing with butter,
Others had fruit cake
As thick as your fist,
Sipping hot tea from
Fine, delicate china,
You'll guess why this cream tea
We cannot resist.

THE RETIRED COUPLE

What caught my eye as they
  passed by,
Was something in their style,
I was impressed, as smartly dressed,
Love trembled in their smile.
Each day I saw the warmth they wore,
So kind the hand he lent,
Heads bent to cloak a secret joke,
Careless to where they went.

I felt bemused, the care he used,
To help her cross the road,
The tenderness of gentleness,
From him to her bestowed.
I knew I stared, for love they shared,
Glowing from shining eyes,
Lips to her ear, what she could hear,
Caused a sweet blush to rise.

Each day at four they'd cross
  the moor,
Privileged I was to see,
This golden couple, arms entwined,
Returning home to tea.
Then suddenly I didn't see
Them walking as before,
As days passed by, with anxious sigh,
I saw my pair no more.

Then one warm day he passed my way,
Something about his head,
Eyes lifted high towards the sky,
Told me his love was dead.
A sadness pressed inside my breast,
As questions filled my mind,
Did they both know that she would go,
And leave her love behind?

I glanced to see, full of pity
For this sad, lonely man,
Then startled saw, the look he wore,
-I'll explain if I can.
His face alert, eyes without hurt,
Contented he passed by,
He seemed to hear and feel her near,
Her presence could not die.

He saw the things, birds on swift wings,
The hedges full of bloom,
She loved them all, things great
  and small,
The insects, flowers and broom.
It was the same, he heard her name
In every pigeons coo,
He saw her smile at every style,
As lapwings rose and flew.

So face aglow in sun and snow,
With her he goes walks still,
He knows she's there, in sea and air,
Leave him, she never will.

FRUSTRATION

I swept the leaves up thoroughly,
And weeded everywhere,
I edged the lawn and mowed it with
Such diligence and care.

Removing all dead flower heads,
It looked so spick and span,
I watered all my special plants,
Wielding my watering can.

I should have realised of course,
It was a gardener's fate,
That night there'd be a great rain storm,
Whose winds would not abate.

It tossed down branches, nuts and twigs,
Attacked each bush and leaf,
The debris that it left behind,
Filled me with unbelief.

The lawns were splattered, flowers bent,
Water lay everywhere,
My garden chairs lay upside down,
It really was unfair.

Gritting my teeth, I took the broom,
And slaved till all was done,
Agreeing that a gardener's lot,
Is a frustrating one.

MY BEATITUDES

I know I am blessed
For I'm trying to be
A purely unselfish
And God-loving me,
I'm trying to lose all
The self that's no good,
Behave in the way that
I know that I should.

I know that I'm blessed
For I've conquered my grief,
The fact we live on
Brings me so much relief,
It's comfort to know that
I have tried my best,
That life's in God's hands
And that He'll do the rest.

I know I am blessed
For I've promised to be
Aware of my faults, which
I don't always see,
For as I've progressed
Now I constantly feel,
A presence upholds me,
It's Godly but real.

I'm blessed for my hunger
For truth is fulfilled,
And wisdom and knowledge
Is being distilled
To aid my new growth
And to show me the way,
To guide what I write
And to curb what I say.

I'm blessed for my senses
Teach me how to live,
To know when to help and
When comfort to give,
Affected by others
My feelings are moved,
In my understanding,
My doubts are disproved.

But I am still blessed
When pain shadows my day,
It makes me look inward
Without more delay,
For often it's unease
That's causing this pain,
So I will trust God
Till I'm well once again.

I'm blessed that injustice
In life sought me out,
That faults and deceitfulness
I learned about,
I had to be taught how
To see through the bad,
And know there's a lesson
In traumas I've had.

For positive thoughts will
Set your spirits free,
Some things don't seem good
But are testings you'll see,
Again and again you
Will say to a friend,
What a silly to worry
It worked out in the end!

BROLLY BATTLE

It poured down with rain
As we started to walk,
I grabbed the umbrella,
Absorbed in our talk,
We laughed as we chattered,
Now covered and dry.
Our day had been great
But the hours had flown by.

She couldn't get into
The car I espied,
I gave her the brolly,
"Don't get wet," I cried.
She stood snug and dry
As I reversed the car,
With unfurled umbrella
She couldn't get far.

A battle took place
As she stood in the rain,
It folded, collapsed,
Then it opened again,
I heard, "It won't close!"
Then I knew she'd get wet,
My offer of rescue,
I'd like to forget.

She clambered inside
As I started to fight,
Both helpless we giggled,
I couldn't do right.
Unyielding to tugging,
I pulled and I pushed,
My open umbrella
Resisted, - I blushed.

She burst into laughter,
I struggled and muttered,
At last it surrendered,
We chuckled and spluttered,
Had my car been large
I'd not feel such a Ninny,
But oh, what a game in
My little old Mini!

A SUMMER PLACE

We walked in meadows deep in buttercups,
And hand in hand smiled in delighted glee,
For there were trees, bird song and insect hum,
And nature filled our day with gaiety.

We picnicked dreaming, drunk with summer heat,
As tireless hours sped by on silent wings,
We bared our feet and cooled them in the stream,
And laughed and loved and whispered secret things.

As skimming swallows shared our well-loved place,
Soft breezes swayed the peacock butterfly,
We vowed we would one day come back again,
For this was just farewell and not goodbye.

SWEET DREAMS

The satellite dish is fitted,
The new one that we've bought,
Cliff's getting so excited for
Tonight there's lots of sport.

With such a lot of programmes,
He won't know which to choose,
But how I hope for all our sakes,
His special team won't lose.

All day he's smiling, cheerful,
Relaxed, helpful and bright,
Full of anticipation of
The game he'll see tonight.

I've brought a tray of goodies,
To keep his spirits high,
Then dash off to my study as
He waves a fan's goodbye.

I write, revise and print out,
To roars on the T.V.
So glad I am, my darling man
Is watching happily.

Two hours of blissful writing,
I think I'll take a peep,
I gasp, I can't believe it for
He's fallen fast asleep!

TIME FOR YOUR LIFE

Your time spent with God
Is never a waste,
For in silence
He reaches for you,
Whatever you think
Whatever you feel,
God will know and will
Follow it through.

You think that because
You feel you can't pray,
And your quiet time's
Jumbled with thought,
You shouldn't say prayers,
It's wasting your time,
But you know this is not
What you're taught.

It's what's tucked away
Deep down in your heart,
Hidden feelings so
Hard to admit,
Those questions unasked,
The longing for truth,
Are all there when
In silence you sit.

But if you let go
Hand over to God,
Then unwind in the love
You have found,
You'll suddenly feel
Peace filling your soul,
And His light you will
Sense all around.

Just open yourself
To the Source of all life,
Simply ask for your time
To be filled
With love, guidance, peace,
Not worries and strife,
Then you'll use your time
Just as God willed

HOPE

As the door opened wide,
A child's voice cried inside,
"Here she is," and delight filled
  her face,
For as laughing Hope stood,
Now removing her hood,
Warmth and joy and a light
  filled the place.

As she greeted each friend,
With a smile without end,
Folk reacted reflecting her light,
Her warm hugs were returned,
As her touch no-one spurned,
For her love came from realms
  out of sight.

But those hurting and sad,
Thought how could she look glad,
They all knew that her husband
  had died;
For great sorrow she'd known,
But her strength it had grown,
From the time in exhaustion
  she'd cried.

She had fought through her fears,
Through his suffering, her tears,
She had asked for her man what
  was best,
And as sad weeks dragged by,
She'd tried hard not to cry,
As her faith in God's love stood the test.

She had always had hope,
Though unsure she could cope,
She'd accepted what God had
  in store,
And on that heart-break day,
When her love passed away,
She felt help with the pain that
  she bore.

Now she knows he lives on,
All his suffering has gone,
For he's happy and not far away;
That's why friends call her Hope,
For they too know they'll cope,
"For if she can, then I can," they say.

MASTER OF THE HOUSE

Rumbling the purrs now of my dearest Benny,
Beneath my hand his fur coat feels like silk,
Warm and contented together we settle,
Communion unbroken till Benny wants milk.

Agile he jumps stretching out like a tiger,
Lazily ambling, expecting his tea,
Emerald eyes turn to demand obeyance,
Telepathy's there between Benny and me.

Sitting in charge of the whole situation,
Unblinking eyes watch as I take his tin,
Patient at first as his meal is got ready,
The cat food that all his affections can win.

Pungent the smell of his delicious tea-time,
Rubbing my legs now, encircling my feet,
Currying favour, impatient but purring,
He knows very soon he is in for a treat.

Licking his lips as his appetite's sated,
Back to the blaze of a warm, glowing fire,
Closing his eyes, in his cat sleep he twitches,
Now dreaming the cat dreams all felines desire.

Restless he wakes, stretches wanting to wander,
Jumps on the window sill spotting a bird,
Fresh for the chase now he sends out his signals,
I open the door for his message is heard.

Banging the flap he walks in now expecting,
Me to drop everything, sit in my chair,
Until I do, bolt upright, paws together,
His eyes willing me with a bright, piercing stare.

Flicking his tail in annoyance he's saying,
'What a long time to clear-up after tea.'
Restless he prowls - now his back he is turning,
Until once again he can sit on my knee.

Benny, oh Benny, adorable pussy,
Arrogant, naughty, sometimes
  you can be,
Oh how I love you, and oh,
  don't you know it,
That look is triumphant
  you've just given me!

THE BRIDE

Could this really be her?
Was it only a dream?
In the mirror she saw there,
A bride dressed in cream.

She had never believed
She would marry again,
After grief and confusion,
And traumas of pain.

Her reflection she saw,
Was both peaceful and calm,
No expressions of doubting,
No fears or alarm.

She smiled back at herself,
But tears moistened her eyes,
To the past and to suffering,
She said her goodbyes.

She adjusted her hat,
With the large, satin bow,
Took her bouquet and walked
To the car down below.

"You look lovely," she heard,"
Vaguely she gave a smile,
In a very short time
She would walk down the aisle.

Like a slow-motion replay,
The service took place,
And the way he adored her,
Shone clear on his face.

For so late in their life,
They had found a twin soul,
As her broken heart healed
She knew now she was whole.

As they both made their vows,
And their rings were exchanged,
She gave thanks for the marriage,
That God had arranged.

THE RIGHT MOMENT

My hair is wound in rollers,
Shampooed and dripping wet,
Someone will knock on my front door,
Or they'll telephone, you bet!

I try to choose my moment,
To wash my hair in peace,
But from the moment that I start,
Interruptions never cease.

My hair is long and curly,
Controlled it has to be,
And using heated rollers is
An essential thing for me.

I feel so unattractive,
My husband I avoid,
Hoping that in the garden he
Will stay usefully employed.

Oh good he's busy weeding,
I'll wash clothes out of sight,
It should be dry by half past ten,
So at last I've got things right.

Who's talking to my husband?
The vicar! I shall hide
Upstairs until he's gone away,
- Am I vain or is it pride?

I'll hide behind the curtain
- My neighbour's passing by,
I'll hang my washing with bent knees,
Good, my hair is almost dry.

At last I've brushed and combed it,
Silk locks lie 'round my face,
I call out gaily, flaunt my charms,
But admirers? There's no trace!

THE FAWN

What we discovered on that day,
Was a complete surprise,
A valley banked with bluebells veiled
Beneath transparent skies.

A secret, scented hollow glade,
Concealed from public view,
Kept for the rabbits and the deer,
And us the privileged few.

A sound of snapping undergrowth,
Caused us to stop and freeze,
A tiny creature tottered forth,
No higher than my knees.

A baby deer stepped daintily,
Directly where we stood,
We held our breath, standing so still,
As silent as we could.

It raised its head so shyly then
And gave a timid blink,
But as we stared it turned and fled,
Before we'd chance to think.

We smiled and hugged in sheer delight,
When it had gone away.
It was a precious gift for us,
The fawn had blessed our day.

THE STRENGTH TO TRUST

It's so easy to trust
When your life's going well,
And your world's filled with
Hope, love and light,
But when some days are sad,
Filled with worries and pain,
It's so hard to keep up
With the fight.

When you know God is there,
As forever He is,
There is always a strong,
Powerful link,
And by turning your mind
From your troubles to Him,
He will colour the thoughts
That you think.

So don't ever let go,
Of the light that's inside,
Where you know God awaits
When you call,
For He'll lift up your hearts,
And He'll fill you with hope,
When in fear or despair
You might fall.

So have faith, turn to Him,
Just accept He is there,
And whatever the worst
Life can bring,
You'll be filled with His strength,
And His comfort and love,
And you'll know you can
Face anything.

OH TO BE A VALENTINE

I can't help being romantic,
For romance goes to my head,
And even when I'm sensible,
I love sweet things you've said.

A song can stir a memory,
Of our youth, cafes, a place,
A compliment, "How young you look!"
Brings smiles on to my face.

Receiving flowers, a red rose,
Is a most romantic thing,
And unexpected chocolates,
Such pleasures they can bring.

A card on anniversaries,
No reminder, hint from me,
Are pleasures that I love and need,
A thought shown lovingly.

I sigh - the postman's passing,
But I see a work of art,
For on the misted window's drawn,
An arrow and a heart.

I see you've brought no flowers,
But a nice, hot cup of tea,
And as love lies deep in your eyes,
Sweethearts we'll always be.

CINDY

My dear little Cindy,
Oh how we did love you,
For you've been our child,
And the love of our life.
The day that we lost you,
We couldn't believe it,
The hurt was so painful,
As sharp as a knife.

But we know you're near us,
Our sweet little Cindy,
You're watching us, loving us
With your dear eyes,
We know you'll be sad
If we carry on grieving,
So we'll try to smile now
But say no Goodbyes.

For you're only waiting,
Our poodle, dear Cindy,
Not dead but alive
In your new Spirit Land,
You're playing and running,
Enjoying your freedom,
But oh, when we meet again,
Won't it be grand?

For we fell in love at
First sight when we saw you,
Your little face turned 'round,
And then our eyes met,
You had to be ours from
That moment of greeting,
The pleasure you gave us,
We'll never forget.

Although we can't see you,
We know you can hear us,
So we'll speak your name
And we'll talk to you still,
But oh how we miss you,
And wish we could hold you,
It's hard to accept now,
But one day we will.

But there's so much love that
Is stored up inside us,
That there'll be another dog,
For us you'll see,
But never, oh never,
We'll try to replace you,
Another sweet Cindy,
There never could be.

For you we remember
Asleep on the big bed,
Curled up on our laps,
Going walks down the lane,
How you barked with joy as
You trotted, tail wagging,
Be happy dear Cindy,
Till we meet again!

THE DRESS REHEARSAL

The stage has been erected,
And the curtains are in place,
"Well almost!" says my colleague
With a question on his face.
The class-room's crammed
  with shepherds,
Who are tangling up their crooks,
A cry for help, "Some safety pins?"
- "You're dressed, now look at books!"

The angel's wings won't hang right,
And King Herod's feeling sick,
The Wise Man's sash is 'round
  his knees,
- "Help get the bucket quick!"
Joseph has started crying,
For his nerves are all in shreds,
- "The tinsel, have we bought enough
To halo angel heads?"

The manger leg is wobbling,
But Jesus is in the hay,
Then Mary shouts in panic,
"Baby's arm has come away!"
"Miss, Peter's pulled his tooth out,
Oh, Miss come and help him please."
- "Oh dear this gown is far too long,
He'll fall upon his knees."

"Where did I put that paper
Showing where my actors sit?"
- "No we're not ready, Innkeeper,
Just read and wait a bit."
The kings have crooked crowns on,
One of them has lost his gift,
It's found beneath his jersey,
As through cast-off clothes we sift.

The angels now look beautiful,
Their bare feet red - then blue,
"Perhaps you'd better keep on socks.
- They're there inside your shoe!"
The shepherds stop their crook fight,
And the kings look quite serene,
But Mary, Joseph, Innkeeper,
Are nowhere to be seen.

"Have you been to the toilet?
Then into places please.
Where is that list? Ah, here it is.
- Shut the door or we will freeze."
I hurry past a paper chain,
Which drapes around my face,
The closed curtains are not complete.
A mattress fills a space.

"We'll manage for rehearsal!"
But the lighting doesn't light,
"Oh, not to worry," says my friend,
"It'll be right on the night."
My announcer is now ready,
As he reads with skill and grace,
The trouble is the card he reads,
Is in front of his face.

The first entrance is over,
For the curtains had been closed,
But Joseph knocks upon the door,
Where our Innkeeper dozed.
He waves aloft his lantern,
Hitting Joseph on the head,
- "Ouch!" he yells. - His following lines,
Those he should not have said!

The mattress is too thick to move,
So stage hands get no cue,
And starting our important scene,
Mary is in the loo!
The shepherds quite excel themselves,
Their words they shout aloud,
Demure, sweet angels filing in,
- Outside a jostling crowd.

Some minor hitches follow,
Causing panic, laughter, pain,
"This is my last Nativity,
I won't do this again!"
The great day has at last arrived,
The play is a delight,
If only I had listened to
'It'll be right on the night!'

THE AUTUMN OF HER LIFE

Her hair was ruffled in the breeze,
Furry collar pulled up high,
Entranced by autumn's painted trees,
How she laughed! - Leaves fluttered by.

Kicking her feet in crunchy piles,
Stumbling, a leaf she caught;
He watched her antics and her smiles,
'Oh, how young she looked,' he thought.

Startled, she saw him sitting there,
Adoration in his face,
Her blushes and her tumbled hair,
Added to her youthful grace.

Love surged then as she kissed his cheek,
His child-bride in disguise,
Though she'd be seventy-five next week,
She was sixteen in his eyes!

LOOK LIKE A BUS

Oh how confusing the lanes and directions,
Cars rushing past as we searched for the way,
Sign posts obscured and three lanes not signposted,
We must make a decision now without delay.

Impatient drivers annoyed as we lingered,
Trying to know which direction we'd take,
Angry, red faces, loud voices, rude gestures,
Quickly hastened decisions that we had to make.

Into the lane where we could see no traffic,
Pleased that the traffic lights were still on red,
How could we know that we'd chosen the bus lane?
Until realization rushed blood to our head.

A double decker behind us was looming,
And now another was following us,
"Help it's a bus lane and we shouldn't be here,
"What on earth can I do?" - I laughed, "Look like a bus!"

Then how we giggled although we were stuck there,
Somehow the lights knew that we weren't a bus,
They wouldn't change for a car we concluded,
And we couldn't turn 'round! It was awful for us.

Then both our heads we poked out of the window,
Red head and blonde head, we begged for mercy;
Grinning the driver signalled to his colleague,
Very carefully backed so our car was set free.

Thanking the drivers, pink-cheeked we manoeuvered,
Glad we were small not as big as a bus,
Drivers this time smiled at our dire affliction ,
But I bet they were glad there weren't many like us!.

GIFT OF HEAVEN

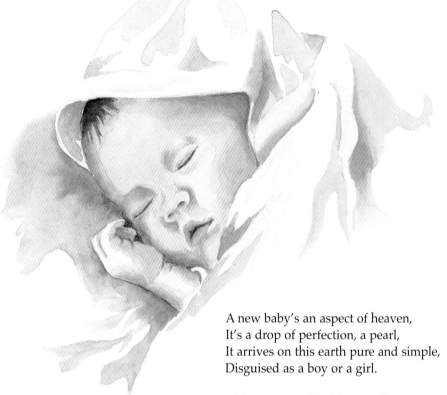

A new baby's an aspect of heaven,
It's a drop of perfection, a pearl,
It arrives on this earth pure and simple,
Disguised as a boy or a girl.

It's a tiny new life, it's a promise,
Brand new hope for a life not yet known,
Its unique little form and its beauty,
Is there to be shared till it's grown.

God has sent this pure, sweet individual,
To bring light to our lives with its charm,
It's a chance to enjoy and to cherish
This gift and protect it from harm.

So before it is touched by the earth plane,
While it's innocent, faultless and true,
Let us cloak it in love and devotion,
So God's child will receive what is due.

DUVET DITTY

Oh good there's lots of duvet,
I'll tuck it 'round my chin,
My back is really freezing,
And a dreadful state I'm in.

It's wedged beneath his shoulders,
I'll grab it very tight,
Then when he next rolls over,
I shall have my half tonight.

Great! Now he's sleeping soundly,
And very still he lies,
I'll snuggle down - how cosy!
But again I'm full of sighs.

The duvet's slipped to one side,
My feet are icy now,
So silently I'll creep out,
And I'll pull it back somehow.

Not sleeping makes me cranky,
And grumpy words are said,
I struggle to retrieve it,
Stub my toe upon the bed.

Because I've now disturbed him,
And draughts cause him distress,
Sad sounds of shocked discomfort,
Don't help me, I must confess.

"I only want some duvet,
It's over on your side!
My generous love surrenders,
Sleepily I creep inside.

Now I've a lot of duvet,
Because I'm holding on,
But any moment I shall hear,
"Where on earth's the duvet gone?"

COMFORT

There's a pathway that leads you to heaven,
And that pathway will lead you through life,
It's surrounded by testings and trials,
By health problems and ageing and strife.

But it's also surrounded by beauty,
By much happiness, laughter and peace,
Satisfaction and service and knowing,
That this life carries on, does not cease.

There is always the comfort of friendship,
The kind person you know understands,
What a wonderful, comforting feeling,
When you place yourself into God's hands.

For whatever the problem to work through,
He will help you with His loving care,
And He'll never, not ever desert you,
As forever and ever He's there.

So keep on, follow your chosen pathway,
Face up bravely to your hurt and pain,
Then what joy there will be with your loved ones,
When one day you will all meet again.

HUGGING

Hugging is a part of me,
That comes so naturally,
It is a loving gesture quite
Spontaneous, full of glee.

Hugging is the way I feel,
An instinct I can't hide,
It's not a sloppy fashion but
A cuddle from inside.

Hugging is a contact with
Kind friends who touch my heart,
My hug's a way of greeting them,
And friendship when we part.

Hugs can show compassion and
Give comfort, love and pleasure,
So when someone gives me a hug,
It's something that I treasure.

Just a few refuse a huge
I smile though I am sad,
And wing it on a prayer to them,
The hug I wish they'd had.

For if my hug's too personal,
Or if they think it's twee,
I hope they'll find forgiveness for
It's the way that God made me.

REBIRTH

I've done it Lord, I'm born again,
I'm whole, complete and free,
I'm filled with strength and love and joy,
That You have given me.

My heart is overflowing Lord,
My head and heart agree,
You've opened up Your loving arms,
To guide my destiny.

My prayers You've answered fully and
Your kingdom's open wide,
I've cast aside my doubts and fears,
You've let me step inside.

I feel Your strength and promise,
Your forgiveness and new hope,
Life's lessons now You'll help me face,
For I know I can cope.

So thank-you dear Lord Jesus,
I want to sing and shout,
Because I know what freedom is,
What joy is all about.

My heart's unburdened and so light,
Alive, I feel so strong,
Because at last my way is clear
To You where I belong.

I ASKED TO SEE GOD

I asked to see God and then what did I see,
Just masses of faces all looking at me,
They mixed and they mingled all races on earth,
As hope made them smile so love gave them rebirth.

The hungry and well-fed shared food with each other,
The healthy gave aid treating each as a brother,
No longer did faith cause diversions and strife,
For weary of fighting, love gave them new life.

The pleading hand outstretched was taken and led
To shelter, to comfort, a warm, cosy bed;
The desperate, the druggies, the sick and the lame,
Were welcomed and nurtured and treated the same.

The lonely, the jail-bird, the girl on the street,
Saw hope in each face and no longer defeat;
For God I saw there in the light, in the crowd,
His spark in each one sent out stars in a cloud

Which melted away as love burst into flame,
Now I saw God there and we all looked the same.
He waits till we recognise Him in each other,
And if we serve God we serve sister and brother,

And as we are all part of God's great family,
I know where I see God, in the whole world and me!

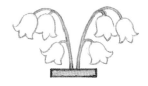